# Cambodian
## Cooking

Joannès Rivière
Photos by Maja Smend

A humanitarian project
in collaboration with Act for Cambodia

PERIPLUS EDITIONS
Singapore • Hong Kong • Indonesia

# Contents

# Discovering Cambodian Food

Many countries, from China to Vietnam and Thailand, have long shared their national and regional cuisines. Cambodia, however, is almost certainly unknown territory for most of us. Its rural areas are the home of a secret treasure jealously guarded by the families who've lived there for centuries—a cuisine that combines authenticity and diversity, simplicity and originality. Now, with this collection of recipes from the young chefs from the Sala Bai School, you have the chance to discover this rich tradition in all its splendor.

Cambodian food is a thousand-year-old tradition. To discover it, you must step back in time to the era of the kingdom of Angkor, the cradle of Khmer civilization, when Cambodian cuisine forged its special identity. Here, cooking is an oral art that has been passed down over time from mother to daughter. It is from this ancestral rite that a traditional cuisine, punctuated by the use of natural ingredients, developed.

Thanks to the influence of other countries, Cambodian cooking has been enriched and expanded over the centuries. China introduced the steaming method and the use of soy and noodles and India introduced curries, to name but two examples. These influences contribute to the particularly wide range of flavors that surprise the palate and stimulate the taste buds. Salty and sweet, and downright bitter and sour, go hand in hand or are blended subtly, sometimes within a single dish, to create a deliciously harmonious and original result.

A Cambodian dish is a feast for the eyes as well as the palate, and the ingredients that compose it are like the colors on a painter's palette: gleaming red chilies, bright green limes, orange shrimp, flecks of pure white coconut . . . the more harmonious the colors, it is thought, the more subtle the flavor of the finished dish.

Visitors are often surprised by the variety and quantity of fish products on the market in Cambodia. In addition to fresh fish, fish pickled in brine, salt fish, dried fish and smoked fish are also widely available. Fish are ground into complex pastes flavored with spices, crab, sticky black rice, vinegar, sugar and even sometimes unripe papaya. The original purpose of these delicious products was to provide a means of preserving the catch from the two major rivers in Cambodia—the Tonlé Sap and the Mekong. Fresh fish and fish products constitute the main source of protein for many families, and also contain valuable calcium, which is essential in Cambodia as there are no local dairy products.

The recipes in this book are simple and easy to produce. They require little preparation time and don't involve any complicated techniques. Most of the ingredients can be found in your local supermarket and the more specific ingredients (including suitable Asian substitutes) can be found at the nearest Asian grocery or on-line.

Ingredient alternatives are provided in the Ingredient section (pages 8–11) and helpful tips are given within the recipes. Together, they will help you navigate this culinary adventure and ensure your success.

Basic cooking equipment can be used to cook Cambodian food at home. However, a mortar and pestle is the best tool for crushing whole spices and making spice pastes. Many of the recipes will specify "pounding" ingredients in a mortar and while a food processor is a sufficient substitute, a traditional mortar and pestle makes quick work with little clean up.

The recipes serve four people as a main course, however they can easily be cut in half to yield a smaller quantity or served with other dishes to feed a crowd.

# Ingredients

**Asian shallots** are small and round and have a pinkish-purple color. Shallots add a sweet oniony flavor and a hint of garlic to countless dishes. They are also sliced, deep-fried and used as a garnish.

**Banana flowers** are the unopened male flowers of the banana plant—a purple-red inflorescence tinged with yellow at the base that hangs at the end of a clump of developing bananas. The hearts of these flowers, which have been stripped off their purple petals, are a popular salad ingredient in some Southeast Asia cuisines. Fresh, canned and dried banana flowers can often be found in specialty stores outside Asia, particularly those stocking Vietnamese and Thai ingredients. Choose a firm, large flower with an even color and check that the outer petals are not wilted. To prepare the flower for cooking, remove the coarse outer petals to reveal the creamy white heart. Quarter the heart lengthwise with an oiled stainless steel knife to avoid the sticky sap clinging to it. If not cooking immediately, soak in cold water or rub with lemon or lime juice to avoid discoloration. Simmer the cut heart in plenty of lightly salted water until tender, about 15 to 20 minutes. Drain, cool then pull out and discard the hard filaments inside each cluster of yellow stamens as they have an unpleasant texture. Cabbage leaves may be used as a substitute.

**Banana leaves** are used to wrap food for steaming or grilling. The moisture and flavor of the banana leaf makes a difference to the texture and flavor of the food, but if you can't find fresh or frozen banana leaf, use aluminum foil. Before using to wrap food, the leaves should be softened for easy folding, either by soaking in hot water for 5 to 10 minutes or briefly heating over a low flame.

**Basil** Two types of basil are used in the recipes in this book: **Holy Basil** is known as *merap prey* in Cambodian and *kaprow* in Thai. This variety, which can reach several feet in height, has a unique smell, that is a combination of sweet Italian basil and geranium. Holy basil is a common ingredient in Cambodian cuisine—it is often added at the end of the cooking in stir-fry dishes or to stuffings. It can be found in most Asian grocery stores, and may be substituted with Thai basil. **Thai Basil**, known as *chie nieng vong* in Cambodian, *horapa* in Thai and *húng qúê* in Vietnamese has a dark green leaf. Its aroma is similar to Italian basil, with a slight aniseed tang. Thai basil is used frequently in Cambodia to flavor salads and soups. Like most basils, it should only be added to the dish at the very last moment, otherwise it will lose its fragrance. Thai basil is available in some well-stocked supermarkets or Asian markets. It will keep well in the refrigerator for a few days. Fresh coriander leaves (cilantro) can be substituted, but the flavor will not be the same. It is, however, a better alternative than sweet Italian basil.

**Bitter Khmer Leaves** This bitter leaf, also referred to simply as bitter leaf or *Sdao*, is often blanched before use to reduce its bitterness. Sorrel leaves are a good substitute, but are usually only available seasonally. However, fresh spinach can also be substituted.

Dried chili peppers

Bird's-eye chili peppers

Geen and red Asian finger-length chili peppers

**Chili peppers** come in many shapes, sizes and colors. Fresh **green and red Asian finger-length chilies** are moderately hot. Tiny red, green or orange **bird's-eye chilies** (*chili padi*) are very hot. **Dried chili peppers**, known as *mate phlao krim* in Cambodia, refer to mild finger-length chili peppers, with their seeds removed, which have been salted and then dried. They must be soaked before crushing, to remove any surplus salt. Dried chilies can be found in most Asian grocery stores, and will keep indefinitely. If necessary, finger-length fresh chili peppers, with their seeds and inner membranes removed, can be substituted.

**Coriander leaves** are also known as cilantro or Chinese parsley. Available fresh, the roots, stems and leaves are all used in cooking. They are strongly flavored, so use sparingly. Available in most supermarkets—but if you cannot find, use regular parsley with a few fresh basil leaves added.

**Daikon radish** is a large, crisp, white-fleshed radish, with a sweet and clean flavor. It is a vegetable that is widely used in Japanese and Korean cooking, and can be eaten raw, or cooked. The skin needs to be peeled or scrubbed before using. Daikon is available from Asian markets and many well-stocked supermarkets.

**Dried Cambodian fish**, known as *trey niet*, is filleted fish that has been cured in salt and sugar and then dried. It has a delicate flavor. Dried fish must always be lightly fried before using. It is available in Asian groceries, but if necessary, it can be replaced by salt cod that has been soaked to remove some of the salt, or with fresh cooked fish.

**Eggplants** used in Asia are generally of the slender, purple-skinned variety, 15–20 cm (6–8 in) long. They are mild and need not be salted before use.

**Fish paste**, or *prahok*, is one of the most dis-

tinctive ingredients in Cambodian cooking. It is fish that has been preserved in salt until it breaks down into a paste. It has a very strong cheese-like smell that many Westerners find unappetizing, but it undoubtedly adds a depth of flavor to Cambodian food. *Prahok* is available in Asian grocery stores and can always be replaced by its Thai equivalent (*nam prik pha*), the Laotian equivalent (*padek*) or by dried shrimp paste (*belachan*).

**Fish sauce**, known as *teuk trey*, is a thin, salty sauce that is made with the juice that is leftover from preparing *prahok*. It looks like soy sauce, but has a very strong smell. Fish sauce is available in supermarkets and in Asian groceries and its Vietnamese (*nuoc mam*) or Thai (*nam pla*) equivalents can be substituted.

**Galangal** is also known in English as Thai Ginger and as *rumdeng* in Cambodia. A cream-colored white root with a distinct flavor that is used to flavor curry pastes and soups. Galangal is very fibrous and therefore must be sliced very fine, cross-wise, before using. It is available in Asian grocery stores and in some supermarkets. It will keep for several weeks in the refrigerator and it also freezes well, either whole or chopped.

**Green mangoes** In Cambodia, the mango season only lasts just one month. The mangoes are usually not left to ripen, but are used when still green, either in a salad or sprinkled with salt and chili. They can also be used to tenderize meat. Green mangoes can be puchased in Asian and Indian markets, and sometimes supermarkets.

**Green peppercorns** These perishable pep-

percorns are available packed in brine or water in jars or freeze-dried. The green peppercorn is the soft unripe berry, and is less pungent than the riper black and white peppercorns.

**Jicama**, known in Cambodian as *pek koa* and in much of the rest of Southeast Asia as *bengkuang*, is a root vegetable with milky white flesh. In Cambodia, it is eaten on its own, in salads, or with a mixture of salt, sugar and chili peppers. The larger specimens are sometimes used to make a stock or soup. Jicama is found in most supermarkets but can be substituted with a mild variety of apple, such as Golden Delicious.

**Kaffir lime leaves** are known as *kroy saoch* in Cambodia. They are dark green and glossy and are used very much like bay leaves are used in Western cooking. Kaffir lime leaves are added to curries or, the central vein is removed and the leaves are sliced very finely and added to salads and stir-fries where they contribute wonderful fragrance, interesting texture and vivid color. Fresh, frozen and dried leaves are available in Asian grocery stores. They will last for several months in the freezer. If you can't find fresh leaves, you can use dried for stews, soups and other long-cooking dishes, though you should use twice as many dried leaves and remove the whole leaves before serving. You can also substitute lemongrass, but the flavor will not be quite the same.

**Krachai,** also known as Chinese keys or lesser ginger, is an unusual rhizome which looks like a bunch of yellowish-brown fingers. it is known as *kchiey* in Cambodian and is specific to Cambodian cooking and its aroma is sometimes compared to lavender. It is often used in curry pastes and gives Amok, a classic Khmer dish, its very special flavor.

**Lemongrass,** known as *slok krey* in Cambodia, is a fibrous stalk with a white bulb at the root end and flat leaves at the top. The tough outer layers are usually removed and the tender white stalk is chopped or sliced and used in curry pastes, marinades and soups. The leaves can be used to make lemon-flavored tea. Lemongrass is available

in some supermarkets and in Asian grocery stores. It keeps well in the refrigerator or it can be frozen (either whole or chopped).

**Oyster mushrooms** are fan-shaped mushrooms that are usually white or grayish-brown in color. They grow in clusters and are sometimes known as abalone mushrooms.

**Palm sugar** is known as *skoa tnaot* in Cambodia. It has a rich caramel flavor that is more complex than that of cane sugar. Palm sugar is made from the sap of the sugar palm tree (Arenga Pinnata). The sap is reduced to a syrup which is then dehydrated. Palm sugar is available in Asian grocery stores or health food stores. For an authentic preparation, bring the sugar to a boil with a little water to make a thick syrup very like the fresh alternative. You can substitute dark brown sugar, but only use half the quantity that the recipe calls for. You can also substitute maple syrup, although you will need to double the quantity that the recipe calls for.

**Pomelo** is a citrus somewhat similar to grapefruit. It has greenish-yellow skin and pink flesh. The pomelo is drier, sweeter and has a much thicker and tougher peel. It is eaten as a fruit or broken up for salads. Grapefruit may be used as a substitute.

**Pork belly** is a fresh cut of meat that comes from the underside of the pig. The same cut is used to make American bacon. It can be purchased at Asian markets or as a special order at a butchershop or meat counter.

**Rice flour** is made from ground long grain rice and is used to make dough and batter,

mainly for desserts. Fresh rice flour was traditionally made by soaking rice overnight and grinding it slowly in a stone mill. The same result may be achieved by grinding soaked rice in a blender. Dried rice flour is available in natural foods and Asian specialty shops.

**Rice paddy herb,** known as *mô am* in Cambodia and *rau om* in Vietnam, has a pungent aroma and is used exclusively in soups, especially Cambodian Sour Soup. It is available in most Asian grocery stores and will keep for a few days in the fridge. Coriander can be used as a substitute.

**Sawtooth herb** is also known as Mexican Coriander and as *chi ana* in Cambodia and *ngo gai* in Vietnam. Its leaves are long, with a serrated edge and its flavor and aroma is reminiscent of ordinary coriander, but stronger. The fresh leaves are used very often in Cambodian cooking, usually added to soups at the end of cooking or to salads. Sawtooth herb can be found in Asian grocery stores and will keep in the refrigerator for up to one week. Substitute fresh coriander leaves.

**Star anise,** known as *pka tian* in Cambodia, is a dried spice that looks like an eight-pointed brown star. Each point contains a shiny seed with the specific smell that belongs to this spice. Star anise is one of the ingredients for Khmer curry, as well as certain soups, and can be found quite easily on supermarket shelves.

**Turmeric,** known as *romiet* in Cambodia, is a rhizome that looks like fresh ginger root, but is smaller and more orange in color. It is often used in curries and stews. Fresh turmeric has a very fruity flavor. Be careful when handling fresh turmeric as the juice stains. Turmeric is available in Asian grocery stores and keeps well frozen. Dried turmeric, often sold ground into powder, can be substituted.

**Water lily stems,** known as *prolet* in Cambodia, are white stems with a pinkish hue, and with channels running down them. They are used widely in Cambodian soups. Before using them, remove the fine white film on the outside of the stem, as one does for the midribs of chard. Unfortunately water lily stems are not available in all Asian grocery stores, but celery makes a suitable substitute.

**Tamarind,** is known as *ampeul* in Cambodia. The tamarind pod is light brown in color and can be quite long—up to 8 in (20 cm). The pod contains sour pulp and hard, shiny seeds. In Cambodia, tamarind is often eaten green (unripe) with a salt and chili condiment, or ripe as it is. The seeds are also ground and added to various sauces. Ripe tamarind pods are available at specialty produce markets and sometimes in well-stocked supermarkets. Tamarind pulp can also be bought separately and will keep for a long time if it is dried.

**Vietnamese mint (laksa leaves)** is known as *chi pong tia kon* in Cambodia and *rou ram* in Vietnam. It is sometimes also called Vietnamese coriander, hot mint or Cambodian mint, though it is not a member of the mint family. Its botanical name is polygonum odoratum. The narrow pointed leaves of this herb are green with light brown markings and its scent is very distinct—both acrid and peppery. In Cambodia this herb is mostly used in soups and salads. Thanks to its major role in Vietnamese cuisine, it can be found in most every Asian grocery store. It keeps quite well stored in the refrigerator. Equal parts fresh mint and coriander (cilantro) can be substituted.

**Water spinach,** known as *trokun* in Cambodia and as *rau muông* in Vietnam, is one of the basic ingredients in Cambodian cooking. It is a water plant with hollow stems and arrow-shaped leaves. The leaves are eaten raw in salad, and the stems can be chopped and stir-fried or used in soups. Water spinach is available in Asian grocery stores, but if necessary, watercress or bok choy can be substituted.

**Winter melon** is a member of the squash family. It is also called ash gourd, ash pumpkin or winter gourd. The white flesh has a mild flavor and is delicious in stir-fries and soup. Winter melon is available year-round in Chinese markets and specialty produce stores. Substitute with peeled and deseeded zucchini.

# Basic Cambodian Recipes

## Chili Coriander Dip

1/2 cup (125 ml) warm water
1 tablespoon palm or dark brown sugar
4 tablespoons fish sauce
3 small red shallots, peeled and finely
  chopped
1 clove garlic, peeled and chopped
1 bird's-eye chili pepper, finely chopped
1 small bunch coriander leaves (cilantro),
  finely chopped

Combine the water, sugar and fish sauce
in a bowl and mix until the sugar completely dissolves. Add the remaining
ingredients and mix well. Set aside for
30 minutes then serve.

Makes 3/4 cup (185 ml)
Preparation time: 20 mins + 30 mins to rest

## Lime Chili Dip

1 small carrot, peeled and grated
2 cloves garlic, peeled and finely
  chopped
2 bird's-eye chili peppers, finely chopped
3 tablespoons roasted peanuts, coarsely
  chopped
1/2 cup (125 ml) lime juice
1/2 cup (125 ml) fish sauce
4 tablespoons palm or dark brown sugar
1 cup (250 ml) warm water

Combine all the ingredients in a bowl and
mix until the sugar has completely dissolved. Set aside for 30 minutes then
serve.

Makes 21/2 cups (600 ml)
Preparation time: 20 mins + 30 mins to rest

## Green Mango Dip

1 small green mango, peeled and grated
2 bird's-eye chili peppers, peeled and
  finely chopped
2 cloves garlic, peeled and finely
  chopped
1/2 cup (125 ml) fresh lime juice
1/2 cup (125 ml) fish sauce
4 tablespoons palm sugar or dark brown
  sugar
1 cup (250 ml) warm water

Combine all the ingredients in a bowl
and mix until the sugar has completely
dissolved. Set aside for 30 minutes then
serve.

Makes 21/2 cups (600 ml)
Preparation time: 20 mins + 30 mins to rest

## Tamarind Dip

1/4 cup (75 g) tamarind pulp, fibers and
  seeds removed
2 cloves garlic
3 bird's-eye chili peppers
2 tablespoons palm sugar or dark brown
  sugar
1/2 cup (125 ml) fish sauce

Combine the tamarind pulp with the garlic
and chilies in a mortar or a food processor and pound or pulse until combined.
Add the sugar and the fish sauce and mix
well. Set aside for 30 minutes then serve.

Makes 1 cup (250 ml)
Preparation time: 15 mins + 30 mins to rest

Clockwise, from top: Chili Coriander Dip,
Green Mango Dip and Lime Chili Dip

Khmer Curry Paste

## Khmer Curry Paste

Known as *kroeung* in Cambodian, this spice paste is the basic ingredient for many dishes. The paste and/or the separate ingredients will keep in the freezer for several months.

3 tablespoons oil
2 in (5 cm) galangal root, peeled and sliced into shreds
2 in (5 cm) turmeric root, peeled and sliced into shreds
2 in (5 cm) krachai or 6 cloves garlic, peeled and chopped (optional)
3 stalks lemongrass, tender inner part of bottom third only, finely chopped
4 small red shallots, peeled and chopped
10 kaffir lime leaves, finely sliced
2 teaspoons fish paste (*prahok*), finely chopped

Heat the oil in a wok or skillet over medium heat. Add all the ingredients and fry until golden brown. Transfer the mixture to a mortar or a food processor and blend into a smooth paste.

Makes 1 cup (250 g)
Preparation time: 30 minutes

## Pickled Vegetables

$1/_2$ cup (125 ml) rice vinegar or white vinegar
1 tablespoon salt
6 tablespoons sugar
1 carrot, peeled and sliced into fine strips
1 daikon radish, peeled and sliced into fine strips
$1/_2$ cucumber, peeled and sliced into fine strips
3 cloves garlic, peeled, left whole
2 bird's-eye chili peppers, coarsely chopped
3 sprigs coriander leaves (cilantro), roughly torn

Combine the vinegar, salt and sugar in a small saucepan and bring to a boil. Remove from the heat and set aside.

Combine the vegetables, garlic, chilies and coriander leaves in a bowl. Pour the vinegar mixture over the vegetables and marinate in the refrigerator overnight. Store the Pickled Vegetables in a glass jar with a tight-fitting lid in the refrigerator.

Makes 3 cups (750 g)
Preparation time: 25 mins + overnight to marinate

## Khmer Fish Stock

1 lb (500 g) fish bones (such as sole, flounder, orange roughy, halibut or tilapia)
1 tablespoon oil
2 in (5 cm) galangal root, peeled and finely chopped
4 cloves garlic, peeled and finely chopped
3 stalks lemongrass, tender inner part of bottom third only, finely chopped
1 onion, finely chopped
1 teaspoon fish paste (*prahok*)
4 cups (1 liter) water
2 tablespoons palm sugar or dark brown sugar
5 tablespoons fish sauce

Rinse the fish bones and chop them roughly into pieces.

Heat the oil in a stockpot and fry the bones until they begin to brown. Add the galangal, garlic, lemongrass, onion and fish paste (*prahok*) and mix. Add the water then add the sugar and fish sauce and stir to combine. Simmer gently for 30 minutes. Strain and discard the solids. The stock will keep for one day in the refrigerator, and for several months in the freezer.

Makes 4 cups (1 liter)
Preparation time: 50 minutes

## Khmer Chicken Stock

1 lb (500 g) chicken bones
1 tablespoon oil
2 in (5 cm) galangal root, peeled and finely chopped
4 cloves garlic, peeled and finely chopped
3 stalks lemongrass, tender inner part of bottom third only, finely chopped
1 onion, finely chopped
1 teaspoon fish paste (*prahok*)
4 cups (1 liter) water
2 tablespoons palm sugar or dark brown sugar
5 tablespoons fish sauce

Smash the chicken bones with the back of a cleaver, then follow the same procedure as for the Khmer fish stock recipe on this page. Simmer gently for 1 hour, strain and discard the solids.

Makes 4 cups (1 liter)
Preparation time: 1 hour 20 minutes

# Snacks and Appetizers

One of the most pleasurable ways to experience a new cuisine is with little bites of food, allowing you to taste a panoply of flavors. Whether you're looking for a satisfying snack or enticing appetizer, you'll find delicious choices in this chapter—from Fish Cakes with Chives and Lime Leaves (opposite) to a Pork Terrine Sandwich, a Cambodian version of the more well-known Vietnamese bah mi sandwich.

# Fresh Salad Rolls with Shrimp

Sometimes called "summer rolls," these elegant rolls are filled with an abundance of tender shrimp and cooling cucumber and mint. Variations of these refreshing rolls are popular throughout the steamy climes of Southeast Asia. Our dipping sauces give them a special Cambodian flair.

**8 dried rice paper wrappers (8 in/ 20 cm in diameter) (see note)**

**Handful of dried rice vermicelli**

**7 oz (200 g) fresh shrimp, peeled and deveined**

**8 lettuce leaves, washed and dried**

**1 carrot, peeled and sliced into very fine strips**

**1/2 cucumber, peeled and sliced into very fine strips**

**2 cups (100 g) bean sprouts**

**1 small bunch mint leaves**

**1 small bunch Thai basil leaves**

**8 green onions (scallions), sliced into short lengths**

Serves 4
Preparation time: 1 hour
Cooking time: 10 minutes

To soften the dried rice paper wrappers, place them between two damp clean dish towels (don't forget to turn them over frequently). They should be soft by the time you're ready to make the rolls.

Blanch the dried rice vermicelli in hot water for 1 to 2 minutes until soft, then rinse with cold water and drain.

Bring a large saucepan of salted water to a boil and cook the shrimp briefly, then plunge them into cold water, drain and set them aside.

To assemble the spring rolls, spread a single soften dried rice paper wrapper out on a clean work surface, smoothing it with your fingers. Place a lettuce leaf, some sliced carrot, cucumber, bean sprouts, and rice vermicelli onto the wrapper, closer to one edge. Fold the closest edge of the wrapper over the filling, then fold in the sides and roll up halfway tightly to enclose all the ingredients. Place a few cooked shrimp, the herbs and a slice of green onion along the roll, then continue to roll up tightly to complete the folding. Repeat with the remaining ingredients and rice wrappers. Set the rolls aside for 10 minutes before cutting.

Slice off one end of each roll for presentation and serve with the Lime Chili Dip (page 12) or Chili Coriander Dip (page 12).

Note: Rice paper wrappers are normally sold dried, and the most common ones you will find in the West are from Vietnam. The best Cambodian rice paper is from the Battambang Provence. These fragile round or square wrappers are made from rice flour and water. Traditionally, batter was spread over a fabric streched over boiling water and steamed. The wrappers are soaked in warm water briefly and then used, uncooked, to wrap spring rolls. They may also be deep-fried. They are available in Asian markets.

# Shrimp Fritters

Lightly seasoned and breaded, these crispy fritters are the perfect start to a meal.

**14 oz (400 g) fresh shrimp, peeled and deveined**
**1 cup (150 g) rice flour**
**4 cloves garlic, peeled and chopped**
**1–2 tablespoons coconut milk**
**1/4 cup (60 ml) fish sauce**
**1 teaspoon sugar**
**3 green onions (scallions), thinly sliced**
**Oil, for deep-frying**

Serves 4
Preparation time: 20 minutes
Cooking time: 15 minutes

Combine the shrimp, rice flour, garlic, 1 tablespoon of coconut milk, fish sauce, sugar and green onions in a bowl. Add the remaining coconut milk if the mixture is too dry, though it should remain thick.

Heat the oil in a large skillet or wok. Drop a few heaping tablespoons of the shrimp mixture into the hot oil. Do not overcrowd the wok (or skillet) or the temperature of the oil will drop. Fry the fritters until golden on both sides, then remove and drain on paper towels. Repeat until all the mixture has been fried.

Serve the fritters immediately with the Chili Coriander Dip (page 12).

**Note:** To test if the oil is sufficiently hot, dip a toothpick into it—if it is covered with tiny bubbles, then it's time to fry the fritters. If not, wait a few minutes more and test again.

# Sweet Potato Rolls with Ginger

These lightly sweetened potato rolls surely reflect the French influence on Cambodian cuisine. Large potato matchsticks are precooked in boiling water seasoned with salt, sugar and copious amounts of fresh ginger. The french fry-like sticks are then rolled up in rice paper wrappers and fried. The best french fries are, after all, twice cooked.

**2 large sweet potatoes, peeled and cut lengthwise into large matchsticks**
**6 in (15 cm) fresh ginger root, peeled and finely sliced**
**Pinch of salt**
**5 teaspoons sugar**
**1 packet small dried rice paper wrappers, 6 inches (15 cm) in diameter (see note, page 17)**
**Oil, for deep-frying**

Serves 4
Preparation time: 40 minutes
Cooking time: 25–30 minutes

Combine the potatoes, ginger, salt and sugar in a pot, cover with water and bring to a boil. Reduce the heat and simmer until the potatoes are just tender, about 10 minutes. Drain and set aside.

Place the dried rice wrappers between two damp, clean dish towels to soften them. Wrap each potato stick in one softened rice paper wrapper.

Heat the oil over medium-high heat in a wok or large skillet. When the oil is hot, fry the potato rolls until golden brown. Drain the rolls on paper towels and sprinkle with salt. Serve hot with the Chili Coriander Dip (page 12) as an appetizer or snack, or sprinkle with sugar and serve as a dessert.

# Pork Terrine Sandwich

This east-west sandwich beautifully melds the flavors of Cambodia with its one time French colonizer.

1 French baguette

$^1/_3$ cup (80 g) Pickled Vegetables (page 13)

1 cucumber, peeled, halved and cut into strips

1 bunch of coriander leaves (cilantro)

**Pork Terrine**

7 oz (200 g) pork rind, finely sliced

1 lb (500 g) pork tenderloin

10 oz (300 g) pork shoulder, chopped

7 oz (200 g) pork liver, chopped

4 cloves garlic

6 stalks lemongrass, tender inner part of bottom third only (see note)

$2^1/_2$ teaspoons sesame seeds

2 tablespoons fish sauce

$2^1/_2$ teaspoons salt

1 tablespoon sugar

To make the Pork Terrine, bring a small pot of water to a boil and simmer the pork rind for 1 hour.

Preheat the oven to 365°F (180°C). Combine all the ingredients for the Pork Terrine in a food processor and pulse until uniformly mixed. Pour the mixture into a mold or casserole dish—the dish should not be more than $^2/_3$ full—and bake for $1^1/_2$ hours. Remove the Pork Terrine from the oven and set aside to cool. Slice into thin slices.

To assemble the sandwiches, cut the baguette into three pieces, then slice each piece in half lengthwise. Fill the slices of bread with slices of the Pork Terrine, Pickled Vegetables, cucumber strips and coriander leaves. Serve immediately.

Note: To prepare the lemongrass, remove the root end and top $^1/_3$ of each piece. Wash the stalks to remove any sand. Peel off the tough outer layers and chop the inner tender white stalk.

Serves 3    Preparation time: 30 minutes    Cooking time: 2 hours 30 minutes

# Marinated Pork Sandwich

This delicious sandwich is the Cambodian version of the famous bah mi, or Vietnamese pork sandwich. Thanks to the colonial era, French bread is ubiquitous in Cambodia.

14 oz (400 g) pork loin, with fat

1 French baguette

Bottled chili sauce, to taste

$^1/_3$ cup (80 g) Pickled Vegetables (page 13)

1 cucumber, peeled and thickly sliced

1 bunch of coriander leaves (cilantro)

**Marinade**

3 cloves garlic, peeled

1 star anise pod

2 tablespoons oil

$^1/_3$ cup (80 ml) soy sauce

4 tablespoons honey

Use a sharp knife to make diamond-shaped cuts in the pork rind.

To make the Marinade, crush the garlic and the star anise in a mortar. Add the oil, soy sauce and honey and mix well. Marinate the pork in a shallow dish or a zip-top plastic bag for 3 hours in the refrigerator, turning it regularly.

Cook the meat on a medium-hot grill, or in the oven at 350°F (180°C) for about 20 minutes, basting it regularly with the remaining Marinade. Set aside to cool and slice it crosswise into slices so that each one has both meat and some fat.

To assemble the sandwiches, cut the baguette into three pieces, then slice each piece in half lengthwise. Spread each piece with a little chili sauce, then fill each sandwich with the Pickled Vegetables, cucumber slices, coriander leaves and sliced pork. Serve immediately.

Serves 3    Preparation time: 25 minutes + 3 hours to marinate    Cooking time: 20 minutes

# Fish Pâté with Peanuts and Tamarind

This flavorful fish pate is a wonderful Cambodian version of a crudité dip—par excellance. Its delightfully compex range of flavors will tempt your taste buds with each bite.

7 oz (200 g) tender white fish fillet, such as whiting, sole or flounder

1 tablespoon tamarind pulp

4 cloves garlic, peeled

$1/4$ cup (45 g) roasted peanuts

1 teaspoon fish paste (*prahok*), finely chopped

3 tablespoons fish sauce

1 teaspoon palm sugar or dark brown sugar

3 green onions (scallions), thinly sliced

Small bunch of holy basil, leaves chopped and stems discarded

1 lemon, sliced

Khmer Raw Vegetable, Fruit and Herb Plate (recipe below), for serving

Grill the fish fillets on a well-oiled grill over medium heat or sear them in a skillet.

Soak the tamarind pulp in $1/2$ cup (125 ml) of hot water until soft, then strain it and reserve the pulp.

Combine the cooked fish fillets, garlic, peanuts and the fish paste (*prahok*) in a mortar and pound into a smooth paste with the pestle. Add the strained tamarind pulp, fish sauce, sugar, green onions and holy basil. Serve with slices of lemon and the Khmer Raw Vegetable, Fruit and Herb Plate.

Serves 4
Preparation time: 30 minutes
Cooking time: 10 minutes

# Khmer Raw Vegetable, Fruit and Herb Plate

A combination of fresh raw vegetables, fruits and herbs accompanies many dishes in Cambodia, especially grilled or roasted meat. A selection of vegetables, fruit and herbs are prepared and placed on the table for diners to choose from. The following is a list of the most common offerings at a typical Cambodian table, but other vegetables and herbs such as celery, green or red bell peppers, green onions (scallions), chicory, fresh coriander leaves (cilantro) and mint may also be used.

Lettuce leaves, rinsed and sliced, or finely sliced cabbage

Bitter Khmer leaves, blanched, chilled and sliced, or sorrel leaves, rinsed and sliced

Thai basil leaves

Coriander leaves (cilantro) or saw-tooth herb

Cucumbers, sliced

Green beans, trimmed

Slender Asian eggplants, sliced

Green tomatoes, quartered

Jicama (*bangkuang*), peeled and sliced

Green mangoes, peeled and sliced

Green papayas, peeled and sliced

Arrange the prepared vegetables, fruits and herbs attractively on a platter and serve as a side dish.

Note: If the eggplant is mature, the skin should be peeled.

Serves 4
Preparation time: 35 minutes

# Soft Boiled Eggs with Herbs

Fresh herbs make the most humble foods a pleasurable break in a day's routine. Cambodians use fertilized duck eggs that are partway incubated for this protein-rich snack, but chicken eggs are a delicious substitution. If you'd like to use duck eggs for this recipe (partially incubated ones will be more difficult to find), use the following boiling times: 7 minutes for unincubated eggs, 20–30 minutes for partially incubated eggs.

**8 large fresh eggs**
**Juice of 1 kaffir lime**
**Pinch each of salt and pepper**
**1 small bunch Vietnamese mint**
  **(laksa leaves), roughly chopped,**
  **stems discarded**

Serves 4
Preparation time: 10 minutes
Cooking time: 3 minutes

Place the eggs in a pot and cover with water. Bring the water to a boil, reduce the heat and gently boil the eggs for 3 minutes.

Combine the lime juice with the salt and pepper in a small bowl and set aside. Place the chopped mint leaves in a serving bowl and set aside.

Break the top off each egg and serve immediately with the seasoned lime juice and chopped mint leaves. Diners should mix each spoonful of egg with the condiments as they eat.

**Note:** It's important to use very fresh eggs for this recipe. To test the freshness of your eggs, fill a bowl with water and gently drop the egg in. If the egg sinks to the bottom of the bowl and lies on its side, it is fresh. If the egg floats, with the pointed end submerged, it is not fresh and should be discarded.

# Fish Cakes with Chives and Lime Leaves

Khmer Curry Paste gives these fish cakes their special Cambodian flair. Grinding the ingredients in a mortar with a pestle is the traditional method for making them, but a food processor can also be used. Just be sure to pulse the machine until the ingredients come together, but mix in the herbs by hand.

**14 oz (400 g) tender white fish fillets, such as whiting, sole or flounder, roughly chopped**

**3¹/₂ tablespoons Khmer Curry Paste (page 13)**

**2 tablespoons palm sugar or dark brown sugar**

**Pinch of salt**

**Small bunch of chives, finely chopped**

**6 kaffir lime leaves, finely sliced**

**Oil, for frying**

**Bottled sweet and sour sauce, for dipping**

Combine the fish, Khmer Curry Paste, sugar and salt in a mortar and pound until the ingredients are thoroughly combined. Add the chives and kaffir lime leaves and mix well. Roll the mixture into a ball and drop it firmly into the mortar to release any air pockets—this will ensure that the fish cakes do not break during frying. Divide the mixture into 8 portions. Roll each portion into a ball and flatten into a patty.

Heat the oil in a skillet over medium heat and fry the patties until golden brown, about 3 to 4 minutes per side. Drain on paper towels and serve with the sweet and sour sauce or Tamarind Dip (page 12).

Serves 4
Preparation time: 30 minutes
Cooking time: 8 minutes

# Salads

With its warm and humid climate, it's not surprising that Cambodian cuisine offers a wide selection of delicious salads, many of which are satisfying one-course meals. In this chapter you will find Cambodian takes on favorite Asian salads such as shredded chicken or green papaya salads, as well as distinct Cambodian creations such as Pomelo and Shrimp Salad, with lemongrass and fresh herbs, or Pineapple and Ginger Ceviche, with a touch of chili peppers and coriander.

# Chicken and Vegetable Salad with Khmer Herbs

This delicious salad features the banana flower, which is important in Cambodian marriage ceremonies.

Juice of 2 limes, divided
1 small banana flower or 2–3 cabbage
  leaves
2 boneless, skinless chicken breasts
Oil, for brushing chicken
1 tomato, deseeded and sliced
1 small carrot, peeled and thinly sliced
$1/_2$ cucumber, peeled and thinly sliced
1 bunch mint leaves
1 bunch Thai basil leaves
1 teaspoon sugar
3 tablespoons fish sauce
2 tablespoons chopped roasted peanuts
3 kaffir lime leaves, finely sliced
1–2 red finger length chili peppers,
  sliced into thin strips

Pour the juice of 1 lime into a bowl and add a little water. Remove the outside petals and stamens from the banana flower. Slice the pale yellow flower thinly, and soak the slices in the lime juice to prevent them from blackening.

Brush the chicken breasts with oil and grill them over moderately high heat for about 5 minutes on each side, or until they are cooked through. Then cut them into fine strips.

Combine the banana flower with the sliced chicken, the vegetables and the herbs in a bowl and mix together. Season with the sugar, the remaining lime juice and the fish sauce and toss to combine. Garnish with the chopped peanuts, sliced kaffir lime leaves and thin strips of red chilies and serve.

Serves 4
Preparation time: 30 minutes
Cooking time: 10–15 minutes

# Green Papaya Salad

This tart refreshing salad is popular throughout Southeast Asia—from Vietnam to Thailand and Laos.

3 cloves garlic, peeled
2 bird's-eye chili peppers
1 tablespoon dried shrimp
Pinch of (preferably kaffir) lime zest
1 small green papaya, peeled and
  sliced into thin strips
$1/_2$ cup (100 g) sliced green beans
2 tomatoes, quartered
1 small bunch Thai basil leaves
1 bunch coriander leaves (cilantro)
  or sawtooth herb, chopped
4 kaffir lime leaves, finely sliced
3 tablespoons fish sauce
1 teaspoon palm or dark brown sugar
Juice of 1 lime
2 tablespoons chopped roasted peanuts

Pound the garlic, chilies, dried shrimp and the lime zest together in a mortar. Add the papaya, green beans and tomatoes and keep pounding until the papaya is completely incorporated. Add the basil, coriander leaves or sawtooth herb and kaffir lime leaves. Mix together and season with the fish sauce, sugar and lime juice. Garnish with the chopped peanuts and serve.

Note: Cambodians typically include pickled crab in their country's version of this popular salad. Pickled crab is omitted here because of the difficulty of finding it in the West. If you can find it, add 1 pickled crab to the mortar along with the garlic, chilies, dried shrimp and lime zest.

Serves 4
Preparation time: 30 minutes

# Pomelo and Shrimp Salad

This elegant citrus and shrimp salad is the perfect choice for dinner party on a warm spring or summer evening. In Cambodia pomelo is eaten in salads or as a simple snack sprinkled with salt or fresh diced chili.

1 pomelo or pink grapefruit, peeled and segmented (see note)
1 tablespoon oil
7 oz (200 g) large fresh shrimp, peeled and deveined
1 cucumber, peeled, halved, deseeded and finely sliced
1 green bell pepper, cut into thin strips
1 small bunch mint leaves
1 small bunch Thai basil leaves
2 stalks lemongrass, tender inner part of bottom third only, finely sliced
2 cups (100 g) bean sprouts
Juice of 1 lime
3 tablespoons fish sauce
1 teaspoon sugar

Break the fruit segments into rough pieces.

Heat the oil in a skillet over medium heat and fry the shrimp until golden. Alternatively, grill the shrimp on a well-oiled grill and set them aside.

Combine the pomelo, cooked shrimp, vegetables and herbs in a bowl and mix together. Combine the lime juice, fish sauce and sugar in small bowl and stir until the sugar is dissolved. Pour the seasoned lime juice over the salad, toss to combine and serve.

Note: To peel a pomelo, cut the rind into seven equal sections by slicing through it vertically with a sharp knife, being careful not to cut into the inner segments. Starting from the top of the cut, carefully peel away the rind to expose the segments. You will now have a citrus-like pomelo fully exposed like a peeled grapefruit. Remove the citrus membrane and separate the segments.

Serves 4
Preparation time: 30 minutes
Cooking time: 10 minutes

# Watermelon Salad

This unusual salad was inspired by a traditional recipe of Buddhist monks that combines watermelon, dried fish and rice. To save preparation time, use seedless watermelon.

1 tablespoon oil

7 oz (200 g) dried salt cod, soaked in cold water for 1 hour then drained, squeezing out all the excess liquid, or dried Cambodian fish

2 cups (300 g) peeled, diced and deseeded watermelon

3 green onions (scallions), finely sliced

1 small bunch coriander leaves (cilantro), coarsely chopped

Juice of 1 lime

Heat the oil in a skillet over medium heat and fry the dried fish very quickly until it becomes a light golden color. Remove the fish from the skillet and drain on paper towels. Pound the fried fish in a mortar or roughly chop it on a cutting board.

Combine the watermelon, fish, green onions and the coriander leaves in a bowl and toss together. Season with the lime juice and serve.

Serves 4
Preparation time: 15 minutes + 1 hour to soak dried fish
Cooking time: 5–10 minutes

# Tart Shrimp Salad with Cilantro and Peanuts

Cambodians make this delicous salad of just-cooked fresh shrimp and crunchy peanuts with ambarella—an acidic tropical fruit with a crunchy texture. Granny Smith apples make an excellent substitute.

1 tablespoon oil

7 oz (200 g) large fresh shrimp, peeled and deveined

3 Granny Smith apples, peeled and coarsely grated or thinly sliced

2 small red shallots, peeled and finely sliced

1 cucumber, peeled, deseeded and finely sliced

1 bunch coriander leaves (cilantro) or sawtooth herb, coarsely chopped

3 tablespoons fish sauce

1 teaspoon sugar

2 tablespoons unsalted roasted peanuts, coarsely chopped

Heat the oil in a skillet over medium heat and fry the shrimp until golden. Alternatively, grill the shrimp on a well-oiled grill and then set them aside. Combine the shrimp, apples, shallots, cucumber and coriander leaves or sawtooth herb in a bowl and season with the fish sauce and sugar. Toss to combine, garnish with the peanuts and serve.

Note: Buy peanuts with their shells; they'll keep much longer than the shelled variety.

Serves 4
Preparation time: 30 minutes
Cooking time: 10 minutes

# Sliced Pork Salad with Herbs

This brightly colored salad combines satisfying salty pork, refreshing herbs, bright lime juice and the crunch of crisp raw vegetables and roasted peanuts. With little cooking required, it's the perfect meal for a warm evening.

7 oz (200 g) pork belly or Boston butt (shoulder) steak, thinly sliced

4 oz (100 g) pork liver (optional)

1 carrot, peeled and sliced into matchsticks

1 red bell pepper, sliced into thin strips

2 tomatoes, quartered, deseeded and sliced into thin strips

1 small jicama (*bangkuang*), peeled and sliced into matchsticks

2 cloves garlic, peeled and chopped

1 small bunch coriander leaves (cilantro)

1 small bunch mint leaves

1 small bunch Vietnamese mint (laksa leaves)

3 tablespoons fish sauce

1 teaspoon sugar

Juice of 1 lime

3 tablespoons unsalted roasted peanuts, coarsely chopped

3 kaffir lime leaves, finely sliced

Heat a dry skillet over medium heat and fry the pork belly or Boston butt (shoulder) steak until crisp. Remove and drain on paper towels. Cook the pork liver (if using) in the rendered fat, remove it from the skillet and drain on paper towels. Slice it finely and set aside.

Combine the sliced pork, liver (if using), vegetables, garlic and the herbs in a bowl and mix together. Season with the fish sauce, sugar and lime juice and toss to combine. Garnish with the peanuts and sliced kaffir lime leaves and serve.

Serves 4
Preparation time: 35 minutes
Cooking time: 15–25 minutes

# Green Mango Salad with Smoked Fish

This colorful salad displays a wonderful contrast of flavors—from smoky and tart to sweet and spicy.

1 cup (200 g) skinned, deboned and
  flaked smoked fish or fresh fish
2 green mangoes, peeled and grated
1 red bell pepper, thinly sliced
2 tomatoes, sliced into thin strips
3 onions, peeled and thinly sliced
2 stalks lemongrass, tender inner part
  of bottom third only, thinly sliced
1 bunch coriander leaves (cilantro)
1 small bunch Thai basil leaves
Juice of 1 lime
3 tablespoons fish sauce
1 teaspoon palm or dark brown sugar
1–2 bird's-eye chili peppers, chopped
2 tablespoons chopped roasted
  peanuts

Pound the smoked fish roughly in a mortar. If you are using fresh fish, fry it lightly in 1 teaspoon of oil until cooked. Let it cool, debone it and then slice it into thin strips.

Combine the fish, mangoes, vegetables and herbs in a bowl and mix well. Combine the lime juice, fish sauce and sugar in a small bowl and stir until the sugar is completely dissolved. Pour the lime juice mixture over the salad and toss to combine. Garnish with the chopped chilies and peanuts and serve.

Serves 4
Preparation time: 30 minutes

# Pineapple and Ginger Ceviche

This unusual ceviche uses pineapple rather than more acidic citrus, requiring an overnight marinade to chemically cook the fish. When the fish is cooked it will become opaque.

**14 oz (400 g) firm white fish fillets (no skin), such as sea bass, turbot, halibut or monkfish, thinly sliced**

**1¹/₂ cups (300 g) cubed fresh pineapple**

**2 in (5 cm) fresh ginger root, peeled and chopped**

**2 tablespoons salt**

**3 small red shallots, peeled and thinly sliced**

**2 bird's-eye chili peppers, thinly sliced**

**1 bunch coriander leaves (cilantro) or sawtooth herb, finely sliced**

Combine the fish, pineapple and ginger in a shallow dish. Sprinkle with the salt. Cover and marinate in the refrigerator for 24 hours.

To serve, combine the marinated fish with the shallots, chilies and coriander leaves or sawtooth herb in a bowl and mix well. Serve with the Khmer Raw Vegetable, Fruit and Herb Plate (page 22).

Note: Be sure to use very fresh fish when making ceviche.

Serves 4
Preparation time: 25 minutes + 24 hours to marinate

# Marinated Beef Salad with Lemongrass

This classic salad with carpaccio-like beef is equally delicious when made with fish. Simply replace the beef with an equal quantity of fresh tuna or salmon and marinate until the fish becomes opaque.

8 oz (250 g) very fresh sirloin steak, cut into thin strips
1 tablespoon oil
1 small cucumber
Handful of green beans, cut into 1-in (2$^1$/$_2$-cm) pieces
1 bunch coriander leaves (cilantro)
1 bunch mint leaves
5 kaffir lime leaves, finely sliced
3 tablespoons coarsely chopped roasted peanuts

**Marinade**
1 teaspoon fish paste (*prahok*)
2 cloves garlic, peeled and chopped
2 in (5 cm) fresh ginger root, peeled and chopped
2 stalks lemongrass, tender inner part of bottom third only, chopped
1 onion, chopped
Juice of 3 limes
1 tablespoon sugar
Pinch of salt

To make the Marinade, pound the fish paste (*prahok*) in a mortar. Add the garlic, ginger, lemongrass and onion and pound until combined. Add the lime juice, sugar and salt and mix well.

Marinate the beef in a shallow dish or a zip-top plastic bag in the refrigerator for 1 hour.

Remove the meat from the Marinade and set it aside, reserving the Marinade. Strain the Marinade into a saucepan over medium heat. Gently simmer the Marinade until it has reduced to a syrup consistency.

To serve the salad, combine the beef, vegetables and the herbs in a bowl and mix well. Drizzle the reduced Marinade over the top and toss to coat. Garnish with chopped peanuts and serve immediately.

Note: Partially freezing the beef prior to cutting it will make it easier to cut into thin strips.

Serves 4
Preparation time: 35 mins + 1 hour to marinate

# Soups and Stews

From the elegant Stuffed Cucumber Soup to comforting Rice Porridge with Fish or nourishing Chicken Soup with Cabbage and Mushrooms, this chapter includes soups and stews for every occasion and taste. Enjoy a Cambodian favorite with Khmer Fish Stew (opposite)—the country's national dish—featuring the classic rich pairing of coconut milk and Khmer curry. Or, for something light on warm days, try the Chilled Fish Soup with Herbs and Rice Noodles.

# Hot and Sour Fish Soup

The slightly peppery-hot Khmer Fish Stock, along with tamarind and coriander leaves, play starring roles in this pleasantly balanced hot and sour soup. Once the stock is made, the soup is relatively quick and easy to make.

1 small winter melon or 2 zucchini
4 cups (1 liter) Khmer Fish Stock (page 13)
1 tablespoon tamarind pulp
5 oz (150 g) water lily stems or 1 large celery stalk, sliced into $1^1/_2$-in (4-cm) pieces
12 oz (350 g) firm white fish fillet such as cod, haddock, tilapia or perch (with skin), roughly chopped
3 green onions (scallions), sliced
1 bunch coriander leaves (cilantro) or rice paddy herb, coarsely chopped

If you're using winter melon, peel it, quarter it and remove the seeds. Slice into large strips. If you're using zucchini, do not peel them—simply halve them crosswise and slice into strips.

Combine the stock and the tamarind pulp in a pot and bring to a boil. Strain the stock into a stockpot and discard the tamarind pulp. Add the water lily stems or celery, the winter melon or zucchini, and the fish and bring to a boil. Reduce the heat and simmer gently for 5 minutes. Add the green onions and coriander leaves or rice paddy herb and serve immediately.

Note: Be sure to remove the transparent skin from the water lily stems before slicing them.

Serves 4
Preparation time: 25 minutes + time for making the stock
Cooking time: 15–20 minutes

# Chicken Curry with Sorrel Leaves

The distinctive flavor of Khmer Curry Paste, when combined with lemony sorrel leaves and rich coconut milk, creates a truly satisfying chicken curry. If sorrel isn't available, fresh spinach and lemon juice can be used for equally delicious results.

3 tablespoons oil

1 chicken (about 2$^1/_2$ lbs/1.25 kg), cut into pieces, or 2$^1/_2$ lbs (1.25 kg) assorted chicken pieces

5 tablespoons Khmer Curry Paste (page 13)

1 heaping tablespoon palm sugar or dark brown sugar

3 tablespoons fish sauce

1 cup (250 ml) coconut milk

5 tablespoons uncooked jasmine rice, toasted and ground to a fine powder

2 bunches sorrel leaves (*siok chou*), finely chopped, or 1 bunch spinach leaves, finely chopped, plus 1 teaspoon lemon juice

Heat the oil in a wok or a deep skillet over medium-high heat and brown the chicken pieces. Add the Khmer Curry Paste, sugar and fish sauce and cook for 5 minutes. Add a little water to moisten the ingredients and simmer for 45 minutes, or until the chicken is tender. Add the coconut milk and the toasted rice and cook for another 5 minutes. Add the sorrel or spinach leaves (plus lemon juice) and serve immediately with white rice.

Serves 4
Preparation time: 20–30 minutes + time to prepare the Khmer Curry Paste
Cooking time: 1 hour 10 minutes

# Stuffed Cucumber Soup

This pretty soup features the delicate flavor of cucumber, whose white flesh absorbs the satisfying flavors of Khmer Chicken Stock and the seasoned ground pork stuffing, creating one delicious melded taste. In Cambodia, bitter gourds (a.k.a. bitter melon) are used in this soup rather than cucumbers.

2 cucumbers, peeled, or bitter
  gourds (bitter melons), unpeeled
2$\frac{1}{2}$ cups (600 ml) Khmer Chicken
  Stock (page 13)
1 tablespoon palm sugar or dark
  brown sugar
4 tablespoons fish sauce
3 green onions (scallions), sliced
  into short pieces

**Stuffing**
1$\frac{1}{2}$ cups (300 g) ground pork (see
  note)
3 tablespoons Khmer Curry Paste
  (page 13)
4 tablespoons fish sauce
1 tablespoon palm sugar or dark
  brown sugar
3 tablespoons flour
1 small bunch holy basil leaves

Remove both ends of the cucumbers or the bitter gourd (if using). Slice into 2-in (5-cm) thick slices. Use a small spoon to remove the seeds. If you're using bitter gourd, sprinkle salt all over the slices (inside and out), leave them for 30 minutes (this will get rid of bitter taste), then rinse in water and drain.

To make the Stuffing, in a bowl combine the ground pork, Khmer Curry Paste, fish sauce, sugar, flour and most of the holy basil, reserving some for garnishing.

To assemble the stuffed cucumber (or bitter gourd) pieces, stick two toothpicks crosswise into one side of a slice. Fill it with some of the pork stuffing, pressing down lightly. Insert two more toothpicks on the opposite side to hold the stuffing in place. Repeat until all the pieces are stuffed.

Put the stuffed cucumber (or bitter gourd) pieces into a large saucepan, then add the Khmer Chicken Stock, sugar and fish sauce and bring to a gentle boil. Simmer for 20 minutes, or until the melon is tender. Remove one stuffed slice and prick it with a toothpick. If it is tender and no juice runs out, the soup is ready. Serve garnished with the remaining holy basil leaves and green onions.

Note: If you cannot find ground pork at your local grocery store, ask your butcher to grind some for you or grind some pork belly or Boston butt (shoulder) steak in a food processor or chop it very finely with a knife.

Serves 4
Preparation time: 30 minutes + time to prepare the curry paste and the stock
Cooking time: 20 minutes

# Rice Porridge with Fish

This comforting dish is found in many incarnations all over Asia.

3¹/₂ cups (800 ml) Khmer Fish Stock
  (page 13)
4 tablespoons fish sauce
1 tablespoon sugar
7 oz (200 g) tender white fish fillet
  (skin removed), such as whiting
1¹/₂ cups (300 g) uncooked jasmine
  rice
1 small bunch coriander leaves
  (cilantro) or sawtooth herb, finely
  sliced
1 red finger-length chili pepper,
  thinly sliced, to taste
Pinch of freshly ground black pepper
2 tablespoons Crispy Fried Shallots
  (see note)

Combine the stock, fish sauce and sugar in a stockpot and bring to a boil. Reduce the heat and add the fish, gently poaching it for 5 minutes. Remove the fish and roughly chop it.

Pour the rice into the stock and simmer for approximately 20 minutes, or until the rice is very tender, almost over-cooked. Return the fish to the pot and mix well. Serve warm, garnished with the coriander leaves or sawtooth herb, chili, black pepper and Crispy Fried Shallots.

Note: Crispy Fried Shallots are a common garnish in many Asian dishes. They are available in packets and jars in supermarkets. To make your own, thinly slice the required amount of shallots and stir-fry in oil for 2 to 3 minutes, until golden brown and crispy. Remove and drain on paper towels If not using immediately, store in an airtight jar to preserve their crispiness.

Serves 4
Preparation time: 25 minutes + time for making the stock
Cooking time: 40 minutes

# Fish and Vegetable Stew

This soup is very versatile and can be made with whatever vegetables are in season.

**³/₄ cup (150 g) uncooked jasmine rice**

**3 tablespoons oil**

**10 oz (300 g) firm white fish fillets (skin removed), such as sea bass, cod, haddock, perch or tilapia, thinly sliced**

**3 tablespoons Khmer Curry Paste (page 13)**

**2¹/₂ cups (600 ml) Khmer Fish Stock (page 13)**

**3 cups (500 g) mixed diced vegetables (such carrot, green beans, etc.)**

**5 tomatoes, halved**

**4 tablespoons fish sauce**

**1 tablespoon palm sugar or dark brown sugar**

Heat a skillet over medium heat and toast the rice until golden, stirring regularly. Pound the toasted rice roughly in a mortar or pulse in a food processor and set aside.

Heat the oil in the pot and sauté the fish until almost opaque. Remove the fish from the pot and set aside. Add the Khmer Curry Paste and fry for a minute or two, until fragrant. Add the Fish Stock, mixed vegetables, tomatoes, toasted rice, fish sauce and sugar. Simmer gently for not more than 10 minutes, then add the fish and cook until heated through. Check the seasoning, adding more fish sauce or sugar to taste and serve immediately.

Serves 4
Preparation time: 30 minutes + time to prepare the stock and the curry paste
Cooking time: 35 minutes

# Chicken Soup with Cabbage and Mushrooms

This soup is traditionally made with only two ingredients—chicken and pickled lemon. In this recipe, vegetables are included to create a soup with more body. Asian pickled lemons are similar to the ones you can find in a Moroccan grocery store, known as preserved lemons, and can be used interchangeably, though with slightly different results depending on what spices, if any, are used in the brine. Preserved lemons are increasingly available at gourmet food markets.

1 tablespoon oil
2 chicken thighs, each cut in two pieces
6 cloves garlic, peeled and chopped
4 cups (1 liter) Khmer Chicken Stock (page 13)
1 pickled or preserved lemon + 5 teaspoons of the brine (see note)
7 oz (200 g) fresh oyster mushrooms, thinly sliced
1 sweet potato, peeled and diced
2 cups (150 g) finely sliced Chinese cabbage (Napa)
15 green onions (scallions), peeled, white part only
Oil
1 small bunch coriander leaves (cilantro)

Heat the oil in a stockpot over medium heat and fry the chicken pieces until golden brown. Remove the chicken from the pot and set it aside. Fry the garlic in the remaining oil until crisp and golden. Remove the garlic from the pot and set it aside.

Add the stock, chicken pieces, lemon and brine and bring to a gentle boil. Lower the heat and simmer for 15 to 20 minutes, or until the chicken is tender, adding water if the stock has reduced too much. Remove the chicken from the pot and shred the meat, discarding the bones, and set aside.

Add the mushrooms, sweet potato and cabbage and simmer until the sweet potato is tender, about 5 minutes. Add the green onions and simmer for 1 minute.

Add the coriander leaves, shredded chicken and fried garlic and serve immediately.

Note: To make pickled lemons, make deep insertions into the peel of a lemon, fill the cuts with coarse salt, place the lemon in a plastic bag, and refrigerate for 24 hours.

Serves 4
Preparation time: 30 minutes + time for making the stock and pickled lemons, as needed
Cooking time: 40 minutes

# Beef Consommé with Star Anise

This clarified beef broth gets its rich flavor from slowly simmered lean beef, which becomes tender during long looking. Beautiful star anise pods, along with palm sugar and coriander leaves, give it an unmistakable Southeast Asian flavor, while soft boiled eggs add depth and body.

**14 oz (400 g) lean beef (shin or shank is ideal), sliced into strips**
**4 eggs**
**4 tablespoons oil**
**10 cloves garlic, peeled and chopped**
**4 tablespoons palm sugar or dark brown sugar**
**4 tablespoons fish sauce**
**5 star anise pods**
**5 ripe tomatoes, quartered**
**1 small bunch coriander leaves (cilantro) or sawtooth herb leaves, finely chopped**
**3 green onions (scallions), thinly sliced**

Put the meat in a pot, cover with cold water and bring to a gentle boil, skimming any froth that forms at the top. Continue to skim until no froth forms. Drain the meat and set it aside.

Place the eggs in a pot and cover them with water. Bring to a gentle boil and simmer for approximately $3^1/_2$ minutes—until they are soft boiled. Run the boiled eggs under cold water, shell them and set them aside in the refrigerator.

Heat the oil in the pot used to blanch the beef and fry the garlic until golden, then remove it and set it aside. Add the sugar and cook until it starts to caramelize. Then add the beef, fish sauce, fried garlic and star anise. Add enough water to cover and simmer over low heat until the meat is tender, approximately 2 hours. As the liquid evaporates during cooking, add more water to keep the meat covered.

Halve the eggs, then add them and the tomatoes to the consommé and cook for another 5 minutes. Add the coriander leaves or sawtooth herb and green onions just before serving.

Serves 4
Preparation time: 30 minutes
Cooking time: 2 hours 30 minutes

# Tangy Ham and Vegetable Stew

Here, as in other Cambodian recipes, tamarind is used to bring a complementary sour accent to other taste sensations. Balanced with a touch of sugar and ham, this curry soup is irresistible.

$^1/_2$ winter melon or 1 zucchini

$^1/_2$ slender Asian eggplant

2 tablespoons tamarind pulp

2 tablespoons oil

14 oz (400 g) ham, sliced into thin strips

6 tablespoons Khmer Curry Paste (page 13)

2 cups (500 ml) Khmer Chicken Stock (page 13)

Pinch of salt

Pinch of sugar

3 green onions (scallions), finely sliced

Peel the melon or zucchini and cut it into sticks, removing any seeds from the melon. Cut the eggplant into approximately $^1/_4$-in (5-mm)-thick slices.

Heat the tamarind pulp in a small saucepan with a small amount of water, then mash and strain it to obtain the juice.

Heat the oil in a medium-sized saucepan over medium heat and sauté the ham and the curry paste. When the ham starts to turn golden, add the stock. Reduce the heat and cook for 20 minutes. Add the eggplant, melon, tamarind juice, salt and sugar and continue cooking until all the vegetables are tender. Serve sprinkled with the finely sliced green onions.

Serves 4
Preparation time: 30 minutes + time to prepare the curry paste and the stock
Cooking time: 50 minutes

# Khmer Fish Stew (Amok)

There are many recipes for Amok—the national dish of Cambodia. The combination of ingredients in this recipe also appears in soups, stews and savory flans. Amok is normally made with nonni leaves, which are famous for their medicinal properties. Swiss chard is a good substitution.

**3 tablespoons oil**

**2 tablespoons Khmer Curry Paste (page 13)**

**14 oz (400 g) firm white fish fillet, such as sea bass, cod, haddock, tilapia or perch, finely sliced**

**3 cups (300 g) thinly sliced Swiss chard leaves, bok choy or nonni leaves**

**2 cups (500 ml) coconut milk**

**1 teaspoon palm sugar or dark brown sugar**

**4 tablespoons fish sauce**

Heat the oil in a wok or skillet over medium heat. Add the Khmer Curry Paste and fry it until it is browned. Add the fish and the Swiss chard leaves and stir-fry until the leaves started to wilt. Add the coconut milk, sugar and fish sauce and bring just to a boil. Serve immediately.

Serves 4
Preparation time: 25 minutes + time to prepare the Khmer Curry Paste
Cooking time: 25 minutes

# Fish Soup with Herbs and Rice Noodles

This chilled soup, made with cooling coconut milk and served with crisp raw vegetables and fresh herbs, is ideal warm weather food. It's also a great option when entertaining because it can be made the day ahead. It's preferable to use a whole fish for this recipe because the fish head imparts great flavor to the soup.

1 teaspoon dried shrimp
One 1$^1$/$_2$-lb (750-g) whole fish or 1 lb (500 g) tender white fish fillets, such as whiting, sole or flounder
4 tablespoons Khmer Curry Paste (page 13)
2 tablespoons oil
1 cup (250 ml) water
$^1$/$_3$ cup (80 ml) fish sauce
1 tablespoon sugar
1$^1$/$_4$ cups (300 ml) coconut milk

**Accompaniments**
Small bunch (4 oz/100 g) dried rice vermicelli, soaked in warm water for 20 minutes until soft
2 water lily stems or 1 small celery stalk, sliced
3 banana flower petals or 1 cabbage leaf, washed and sliced
1 small bunch sorrel or other bitter-tasting leaves, chopped
$^1$/$_2$ cucumber, peeled and cut into matchsticks
2 cups (100 g) bean sprouts
1 small bunch Thai basil
1 small bunch flat-leaf parsley
Lime wedges, for serving
2 green finger-length chili peppers, sliced, for serving

To make the soup, soak the dried shrimp in warm water for 30 minutes, then drain them and discard the soaking liquid. Slice the fish into large pieces. If you're using a whole fish, discard the tail and set the head aside for the soup. Combine the soaked shrimp, the fish slices (including the bones) and the Khmer Curry Paste in a mortar and pound into a paste.

Heat the oil in a large saucepan over medium heat and fry the paste until golden. Add the water, fish sauce, sugar and fish head (if using). Simmer gently for 15 minutes, then add the coconut milk, remove from the heat and set aside to cool. If possible, refrigerate the soup for 24 hours to allow the flavors to marry. Strain the liquid and discard the solids. Alternatively, strain the soup through a cheesecloth and refrigerate the liquid until cold.

To serve the soup, divide the Accompaniments among four bowls. Pour the cold soup over and serve with lime wedges and fresh chilies.

Serves 4
Preparation time: 1 hour 30 minutes + time to make the curry paste and 24 hours to chill and rest (if possible)
Cooking time: 20 minutes

# Stir-fries

Quick-cooking stir-fries are a staple component of most Asian cuisines, and this is true of Cambodia as well. Cambodian stir-fries encompass a unique range of delicious flavors and varying textures--from the spicy Chicken with Dried Chilies and Cashews to Sweet Sour Fish with Green Mango, and from simple but satisfying Stir-fried Beef with Water Spinach (opposite) to Khmer Curry, a fish or chicken stir-fry enveloped in a rich and opulent sauce.

# Grilled Eggplant with Pork

This is a typical dish from the Kampuchea Krom area in the Mekong Delta.

2 slender Asian eggplants
1¹/₂ cups (350 g) ground pork
3 cloves garlic, peeled and chopped
2 small red shallots, peeled and chopped
2 stalks lemongrass, tender inner part of bottom third only, sliced
2 tablespoons fish sauce
1 teaspoon palm sugar or dark brown sugar
1 bunch coriander leaves (cilantro) or sawtooth herb, chopped

Grill the eggplants in a broiler or oven until the skin is black and the flesh is soft. Cut them in half lengthwise, scrape the flesh out with a spoon and chop it roughly.

Heat a wok or skillet and stir-fry the pork, garlic, shallots and lemongrass until golden. Add the eggplant flesh and cook for 2 minutes. Add the fish sauce and the sugar and mix well. Serve garnished with the chopped coriander leaves or sawtooth herb.

Serves 4
Preparation time: 25 minutes
Cooking time: 25 minutes

# Shrimp with Black Pepper and Cilantro

Glistening with a caramelized sugar coating and dotted with coarsely crushed black pepper to balance the sweet, these delicious "black-tie" shrimp are incredibly easy to make. Serve them at a party with toothpicks or serve with rice as a main course.

3 tablespoons sugar
1³/₄ lbs (800 g) fresh jumbo shrimp, shelled and deveined, or fresh lobster meat (tail meat is preferable)
3 cloves garlic, peeled and chopped
2 tablespoons oil
1 teaspoon coarsely crushed black peppercorns
2 tablespoons fish sauce
1 bunch coriander leaves (cilantro)

Heat a wok or skillet over high heat and add the sugar. When the sugar starts to caramelize, add the shrimp or lobster meat, garlic and oil and stir-fry for 2 minutes. Add the peppercorns, fish sauce and coriander leaves; mix well and stir-fry for a few seconds more, or until the coriander is fragrant. Serve immediately.

Serves 4
Preparation time: 25 minutes
Cooking time: 10 minutes

# Chicken with Dried Chilies and Cashews

Oyster sauce, a culinary influence from China, gives this simple stir-fry its underlying rich flavor. Chili peppers add a touch of fiery heat, but being deseeded the heat isn't overshelming.

**5 dried red chili peppers**

**3 tablespoons oil**

**1 cup (150 g) raw cashews**

**2 boneless, skinless chicken breasts, sliced into thin strips**

**3 cloves garlic, peeled and chopped**

**2 in (5 cm) fresh ginger root, peeled and chopped**

**1 green bell pepper, sliced into thin strips**

**1 slender Asian eggplant, sliced**

**4 tablespoons oyster sauce**

**2 tablespoons soy sauce**

**1 small bunch coriander leaves (cilantro)**

Soak the dried chilies in warm water for 20 minutes. Drain them and pat them dry with paper towels. Remove the seeds and cut them into strips.

Heat the oil in a wok or skillet and sauté the sliced chilies and the cashew nuts until the nuts are golden. Add the chicken, garlic and ginger and fry until the chicken starts to brown. Add the bell pepper and eggplant and cook for 2 minutes. Add the oyster sauce and soy sauce. Simmer until the sauce has reduced slightly and serve garnished with coriander leaves.

Note: For all your stir-fry dishes, slice the meat as close to the grain as possible. This keeps it tender throughout the cooking process.

Serves 4
Preparation time: 45 minutes
Cooking time: 20–25 minutes

# Sweet Sour Fish with Green Mango

Tart green mango contrasts with palm sugar to create a wonderfully balanced sweet-sour base for this delicious stir-fry.

2 tablespoons oil

1$^1/_4$ lbs (600 g) firm white fish fillet (with skin), such as sea bass, haddock or tilapia, cut into pieces

10 cloves garlic, peeled and chopped

5 tablespoons palm or brown sugar

4 tablespoons fish sauce

5 tomatoes, quartered

2 small green mangoes, peeled and chopped

Sugar cane (approx 3 in/7.5 cm), cut into matchsticks (optional)

1 small bunch Thai basil leaves

1 small bunch coriander leaves (cilantro)

Heat the oil in a wok or skillet over high heat and fry the fish until golden. Remove the fish and drain on paper towels. Add the garlic to the wok (or skillet) and fry until it is browned. Add the sugar and the fish sauce and continue cooking until the mixture is just beginning to caramelize. Add the tomatoes, green mangoes and sugar cane (if using) and stir-fry for a few minutes. Add the fish, mix well and cook for another 15 minutes over low heat, without stirring again. Serve garnished with basil and coriander leaves.

Serves 4
Preparation time: 25 minutes
Cooking time: 35 minutes

# Pork with Ginger and Green Onions

The flavor of this dish is punctuated by fresh ginger root. In Cambodia ginger is considered to be a vegetable, rather than a spice or an aromatic, and it is cooked very briefly to retain its strong flavor and crunchy texture.

**3 tablespoons oil**

**8 in (20 cm) fresh ginger root, peeled and cut into matchsticks**

**14 oz (400 g) pork loin, sliced into thin strips**

**15 green onions (scallions), white part only, cut into short lengths**

**3 tablespoons soy sauce**

**1 teaspoon palm sugar or dark brown sugar**

**1 small bunch holy basil leaves**

Heat the oil in a wok or skillet over medium heat and sauté the ginger until it is transparent, approximately 1 minute. Turn the heat up to medium-high and add the pork. Stir-fry until the pork begins to brown. Add the green onions, soy sauce and the sugar and stir-fry for 1 minute more. Add the holy basil leaves and serve.

Serves 4
Preparation time: 25 minutes
Cooking time: 10–12 minutes

# Khmer Curry

Curry is a traditional Cambodian dish served on every important ceremonial occasion. Cambodian curries are distinct in Asia for their use of sweet potatoes. Dried chilies from Cambodia don't tend to be as fiery hot as other dried chilies; if you use them for the Spice Paste, you should add twice the amount specified in the recipe.

1/4 cup (60 ml) oil

2 tablespoons annatto seeds
  (optional, see note)

1 lb (500 g) firm white fish fillets,
  such as sea bass, haddock, cod,
  perch or tilapia, or chicken or beef,
  cut into large chunks

5 fresh kaffir lime leaves or 10 dried
  leaves

2 carrots, peeled and sliced into
  rounds

1 sweet potato, peeled and sliced

1 onion, peeled and quartered

4 tablespoons fish sauce

1 tablespoon palm sugar or dark
  brown sugar

3/4 cup (100 g) green beans, ends
  trimmed and cut into 1 1/2-in
  (4-cm) pieces

1 slender Asian eggplant, sliced

2 cups (500 ml) coconut milk

**Spice Paste**

4 star anise pods

1 teaspoon coriander seeds

1 1/4 cups (25 g) dried red finger-
  length chili peppers, soaked in
  water for 20 minutes then drained,
  deseeded and sliced

1 teaspoon dried shrimp paste

4 tablespoons Khmer Curry Paste
  (page 13)

To make the Spice Paste, combine the star anise and coriander seeds in a small skillet and toast them over medium heat until fragrant. Transfer the toasted spices to a mortar and pound them into a fine powder. Add the soaked chilies, dried shrimp paste and the Khmer Curry Paste and pound into a fine paste.

Heat the oil in a wok (or skillet) over medium heat and add the annatto seeds. When the oil starts to smoke and has a red color, strain it and return the red oil to the wok or skillet, discarding the seeds.

Heat the red oil over medium-high heat and fry the fish until cooked through. Remove the fish and drain it on paper towels. Add the Spice Paste to the wok (or skillet) and fry it until it is lightly browned and fragrant. Reduce the heat to medium and add the kaffir lime leaves, carrots, sweet potato, onion, fish sauce and sugar. Mix well and add a little water to moisten. Stir-fry for 10 minutes or until the vegetables are almost tender. Add the green beans, eggplant and the fried fish and cook for another 5 minutes. Add the coconut milk and bring to a boil. Check the seasoning, adding more fish sauce or sugar to taste, remove the dried kaffir lime leaves (if used), and serve immediately.

Note: Annatto seeds are used as a natural food coloring. The dark reddish-brown seeds are soaked in warm water or fried in oil to extract their brick red color, then discarded. Annatto seeds are sold in plastic packets in Asian specialty stores.

Serves 4
Preparation time: 1 hour 10 minutes + time to prepare the curry paste
Cooking time: 45 minutes

# Stir-fried Fish with Lemongrass and Herbs

This citrus-flavored stir-fry is fortified with peanuts, which grow easily in Cambodia's warm climate.

**3 tablespoons oil**

**1 lb (500 g) firm white fish fillets (without skin), such as sea bass, haddock or tilapia, roughly chopped**

**5 cloves garlic, peeled and chopped**

**1 stalk lemongrass, tender inner part of bottom third only, finely chopped**

**1 small bunch Thai basil leaves, finely chopped**

**6 kaffir lime leaves leaves, finely chopped**

**1 tablespoon palm sugar or dark brown sugar**

**3 tablespoons fish sauce**

**4 tablespoons unsalted roasted peanuts**

Heat the oil in a wok or a skillet over medium-high heat and stir-fry the fish and the garlic until the fish is nearly opaque. Add the chopped herbs, sugar, fish sauce and peanuts and stir-fry for 1 or 2 minutes more, until the sauce reduces slightly, and serve.

Serves 4
Preparation time: 30 minutes
Cooking time: 15 minutes

# Pork with Cambodian Herbs

This simple, delicious dish is a combination of ground meat, fresh herbs, fish sauce and toasted ground rice. Lao and Thai varieties include other ingredients, but the basic recipe is the same.

$3/4$ cup (150 g) uncooked jasmine rice
2 tablespoons oil
$1^1/_2$ cups (300 g) ground pork
3 cloves garlic, chopped
2 small red shallots, peeled and chopped
3 stalks lemongrass, tender inner part of bottom third only, sliced
3 cups (150 g) bean sprouts
3 tablespoons fish sauce
1 tablespoon sugar
5 kaffir lime leaves, thinly sliced
1 bunch mint leaves
1 bunch coriander leaves (cilantro)
1 bunch Vietnamese mint (laksa leaves)

Heat a wok or skillet over medium heat and add the rice. Stir the rice constantly, until it is golden brown. Remove the toasted rice from the wok (or skillet) and pound it in a mortar or grind it coarsely in a food processor.

Heat the oil in the wok (or skillet) over medium-high heat and stir-fry the pork, garlic, shallots and lemongrass until the meat starts to brown. Add the bean sprouts and the toasted rice. Cook for 1 minute then add the fish sauce, sugar, kaffir lime leaves and the herbs. Stir-fry 1 minute more, then serve.

Serves 4
Preparation time: 30 minutes
Cooking time: 20 minutes

# Pepper Crab

The flavor of fresh crab shines in this classic yet simple Cambodian dish. It hails from Kep, a once famous beach town that is known for its fresh seafood, particularly crab, and from Kampot, a nearby inland town best known for its famous pepper, which is still available throughout Cambodia. Thus the dish is sometimes called Kampot Pepper Crab. Some versions use fresh green peppercorns instead of black ones.

**3 lbs (1.5 kg) fresh crabs**
**4 tablespoons oil**
**4 cloves garlic, peeled**
**1 heaping teaspoon coarsely ground black pepper**
**4 tablespoons soy sauce**
**1 tablespoon sugar**
**A few Italian parsley or basil leaves**

Wash the crabs under running water. Place them on a board (belly side up) and use a large knife with a firm blade to quarter them. Remove the claws and split them open by tapping them lightly with the knife. Remove the last segment of the legs.

Heat the oil over medium-high heat in a wok or skillet. Add the crab and stir-fry until all the juices have been released. Add the garlic and pepper, and continue cooking until everything turns golden brown. Add the soy sauce, sugar and parsley or basil leaves and stir until the sauce reduces slightly, then serve.

Serves 3–4
Preparation time: 25 minutes
Cooking time: 25 minutes

# Chicken with Bell Peppers and Basil

With its distinctive flowery perfume, holy basil adds an enticing aroma to this slightly spicy stir-fry. It is the variety traditionally used in classic stir-fry recipes such as chicken with basil.

3 tablespoons oil

2 boneless, skinless chicken breasts, sliced into thin strips

2 bird's-eye chili peppers, chopped

3 tablespoons Khmer Curry Paste (page 13)

1 red bell pepper, sliced into strips

1 green bell pepper, sliced into strips

1 bunch of holy basil leaves

1 teaspoon palm sugar or dark brown sugar

3 tablespoons fish sauce

Heat the oil in a wok or skillet and fry the chicken, chopped chilies and Khmer Curry Paste until the chicken turns golden brown. Add the bell pepper and continue cooking for another 2 minutes. Add the holy basil leaves, sugar and the fish sauce and mix well. Cook until the sauce has reduced slightly and serve.

Serves 4
Preparation time: 25 minutes + time to prepare the curry paste
Cooking time: 20 minutes

# Stir-fried Beef with Water Spinach

This delicious and easy-to-make stir-fry of tender beef and fresh greens requires few ingredients. As in many Cambodian dishes, it is sweetened slightly with a touch of palm sugar.

**3 tablespoons oil**

**14 oz (400 g) boneless beef, sliced against the grain into thin strips**

**2 cloves garlic, peeled and chopped**

**3 small red shallots, peeled and chopped**

**8 oz (250 g) water spinach, watercress or bok choy, cut into short lengths**

**3 tablespoons soy sauce**

**1 teaspoon palm sugar or dark brown sugar**

Heat the oil in a wok or skillet and stir-fry the beef, garlic and shallots until the meat starts to brown. Add the water spinach and stir-fry for 1 minute. Add the soy sauce and sugar and mix well. Cook until the sauce has reduced slightly and serve.

**Note:** Partially freezing the beef prior to cutting it will make it easier to cut into thin strips.

Serves 4
Preparation time: 25 minutes
Cooking time: 15 minutes

# Vegetable Fried Rice

This dish, one of the most basic and essential in Cambodian cuisine, is a popular street food. Fried rice is often eaten as a main dish, but it can be served on the side as well. For a non-vegetarian version, just add bits of pork, fish, chicken or shrimp and stir-fry them with the vegetables before adding the rice.

2 tablespoons oil
3 cloves garlic, peeled and chopped
1 green bell pepper, finely chopped
Handful of green beans, ends
  removed and sliced
1 small carrot, peeled and cut into
  thin strips
1 small turnip, peeled and cut into
  thin strips
4 cups (400 g) cold cooked jasmine
  rice, preferably day-old rice
4 tablespoons fish sauce
1 tablespoon sugar
3 green onions (scallions), thinly
  sliced
1 small bunch coriander leaves
  (cilantro), finely chopped
A few celery leaves, finely chopped
Bottled chili sauce (optional),
  to serve (see note)

Heat the oil over medium-high heat in a wok or skillet. Add the garlic, green bell pepper, green beans, carrot and daikon radish and stir-fry for a few minutes, or until the vegetables begin to soften. Add the rice and stir-fry until it starts to turn golden. Add the fish sauce, sugar, green onions, coriander and celery leaves, and mix well. Serve with chili sauce, if desired.

Note: Chili sauce is a blend of chili and water, seasoned in salt, sugar, garlic and vinegar. It is not thick and has a sweet and sour taste. It is available in bottles in food stores.

Serves 4
Preparation time: 30 minutes + time to cook and cool the rice
Cooking time: 15 minutes

# Coconut Ham Curry with Pineapple

Coconut is one of the basic ingredients in Cambodian cuisine. It is used in everything from curries and soups to desserts. Canned coconut milk is readily available in the grocery store—just be sure to select a variety that doesn't contain any additional sweetener.

1 tablespoon tamarind pulp

1 cup (250 ml) water

4 tablespoons oil

1$^1/_4$ lbs (600 g) ham, diced

4 tablespoons Khmer Curry Paste (page 13)

1 small pineapple, peeled, cored and sliced into 2-in (5-cm) cubes

3 tablespoons fish sauce

1 slender Asian eggplant, cut into matchsticks

1$^1/_3$ cups (330 ml) coconut milk

1 small bunch Thai basil leaves

Combine the tamarind pulp and the water in a small saucepan and bring to a boil. Strain the water and set it aside.

Heat the oil in a wok or deep skillet over medium heat and fry the ham and the Khmer Curry Paste until lightly browned. Add the pineapple, tamarind water and fish sauce, cover and cook for 1 hour over low heat. Add the eggplant and cook for another 10 minutes. Add the coconut milk and bring to a boil and check the seasoning. Add more fish sauce, if desired. Serve garnished with the Thai basil leaves.

Serves 4
Preparation time: 25 minutes + time to prepare the curry paste
Cooking time: 1 hour 20 minutes

# Squid with Green Peppercorns

Mild green peppercorns are a common ingredient in Cambodian cuisine. They're generally cut into small clusters and served with seafood, as here, or with fish or meat.

**14 oz (400 g) fresh baby squid, cleaned and sliced**

**3 tablespoons oil**

**3 cloves garlic, peeled and chopped**

**1 stalk lemongrass, tender inner part of bottom third only, chopped**

**1¼ cups (200 g) green beans, trimmed and sliced**

**5 kaffir lime leaves, finely sliced**

**½ cup (100 g) fresh green peppercorns, cut into small clusters**

**3 tablespoons fish sauce**

**1 teaspoon palm sugar or dark brown sugar**

**1 small bunch Thai basil leaves**

Heat a wok or skillet over medium-high heat and stir-fry the squid for only 20 seconds, or until they release their moisture. Remove the squid from the wok (or skillet) and set it aside.

Add the oil to the wok (or skillet) and stir-fry the garlic and lemongrass for a minute or two. Add the green beans, kaffir lime leaves and the green peppercorns, and stir-fry for 1 minute. Return the squid to the wok (or skillet) and add the fish sauce and sugar and stir-fry for 1 minute more. Add the basil leaves and serve.

Serves 4
Preparation time: 35 minutes
Cooking time: 5 minutes

# Barbecues and Roasts

Whether your taste is for pork, beef or chicken, you will find recipes in this chapter for creating tender, finger-licking good meat and poultry dishes for picnics, backyard barbecues or elegant dinners. The Cambodian knack for combining distinctive yet complementary flavors shines in recipes like Soy Glazed Spare Ribs with Star Anise, Barbecued Beef Skewers and Honey Glazed Chicken, where food is sweetened with palm sugar or honey, brightened with lemongrass or kafir lime leaves, and seasoned with a touch of soy sauce or pungent fish paste.

# Honey Glazed Chicken

In the countryside, Cambodians use an earthenware pot (usually made in the Kampong Chnang area) to cook this dish. They place it on a small barbecue to give the chicken a smokey flavor. The alcohol content of the rice wine allows the herbs and spices to release their flavors gently while the meat remains tender.

**5 tablespoons honey**
**Pinch of salt**
**1 chicken (2$^1$/$_4$ lbs/1 kg), washed and patted dry**
**10 stalks lemongrass, tender inner part of bottom third only, roughly chopped**
**20 fresh kaffir lime leaves or 30 dried leaves**
**10 small red shallots, peeled**
**10 cloves garlic, peeled**
**2 cups (500 ml) rice wine or sake**

Combine the honey and the salt in a small bowl and mix well. Rub the chicken with this mixture and set it aside.

Line a casserole dish large enough to accommodate the chicken with aluminum foil. Scatter the chopped lemongrass, kaffir lime leaves, shallots and garlic in the dish. Heat briskly until the bottom starts to change color. Add the chicken, reduce the heat and cover. Cook for 5 minutes, then add a little of the rice wine. Cook in the covered pan for 1 hour, turning the chicken regularly and gradually adding more rice wine.

Discard the lemongrass, kaffir lime leaves, shallots and garlic. Carve the chicken, place on a platter and serve with Chili Coriander Dip (page 12) and Khmer Raw Vegetable, Fruit and Herb Plate (page 22).

Serves 4
Preparation time: 30 minutes
Cooking time: 1 hour 10 minutes

# Soy Glazed Spare Ribs with Star Anise

Those who enjoy the flavor of anise seeds will appreciate the pronounced licorice overtones in star anise pods, which have a beautiful star-shaped form. Balanced in a sweet and garlicky soy marinade, the enticing flavor of star anise is wonderful foil for these tender spare ribs.

2$^{1}/_{4}$ lbs (1 kg) pork spare ribs
6 star anise pods
4 cloves garlic, peeled
4 tablespoons palm sugar or dark
  brown sugar or honey
$^{1}/_{2}$ cup (125 ml) soy sauce

Serves 4
Preparation time: 25 minutes + 1$^{1}/_{2}$ hours
to marinate
Cooking time: 10–15 minutes

Cut the spare ribs into three pieces. Use a sharp knife to make diamond pattern in the pork to help the marinade penetrate the meat.

To make the marinade, combine the star anise and garlic in a mortar and pound into a paste. Add the sugar or honey and soy sauce and mix well. Marinate the ribs in this mixture for at least 1$^{1}/_{2}$ hours.

Grill the spare ribs over medium heat for 15 minutes, turning them regularly and basting with the leftover marinade. Alternatively, roast them in the oven for 10 minutes at 350°F (180°C), basting periodically with the leftover marinade.

# Barbecued Beef Skewers

In this recipe tender sirloin is infused with the addictive flavor combination of fresh lemongrass, shallots, garlic, soy sauce and a touch of sugar. Because the beef pieces are small, they will cook quickly. Be careful not to over cook them.

**1 teaspoon ground black pepper**
**1 stalk lemongrass, tender inner part of bottom third only, chopped**
**3 cloves garlic, peeled and chopped**
**2 shallots, peeled and chopped**
**4 tablespoons soy sauce**
**2 tablespoons palm sugar or dark brown sugar or honey**
**14 oz (400 g) sirloin beef, cut into 2-in (5-cm) pieces**
**Bamboo skewers, soaked in water**

To make the marinade, combine the pepper, lemongrass, garlic and shallots in a mortar and pound into a fine paste. Add the soy sauce and the sugar or honey and mix well.

Skewer the beef and marinate it for 1 hour in a shallow dish. Grill the kebabs or broil them in the oven for approximately 5 to 6 minutes on each side, basting them with the leftover marinade.

Serve with Green Papaya Salad (page 29) and French bread.

Serves 4
Preparation time: 35 minutes + 1 hour to marinate
Cooking time: 10–12 minutes

# Seasoned Barbecued Pork

These delicious pork patties—typical Cambodian picnic fare—can be enjoyed either hot or cold.

**1 lb (500 g) ground pork**
**3 tablespoons fish paste (*prahok*)**
**4 cloves garlic, peeled and chopped**
**2 shallots, peeled and chopped**
**3 stalks lemongrass, tender inner
  part of bottom third only, chopped**
**Pinch of salt**
**1 tablespoon palm sugar or dark
  brown sugar or honey**
**6 kaffir lime leaves, finely sliced**
**A few banana leaves or aluminum foil**

Combine the pork, fish paste (*prahok*), garlic, shallots and lemongrass in a food processor and grind into a paste. Add the salt, sugar or honey and kaffir lime leaves and mix until just combined.

Place a banana leaf or a piece of aluminum foil on a clean work surface. Place a little of the pork mixture in the middle and fold the leaf or foil to make a small rectangular packet. Cut a second strip of banana leaf or foil the same width as the packet. Wrap the second strip around the packet the other way and secure with a toothpick.

Grill the packets for 15 minutes over medium heat, turning them regularly, or bake them in the oven for about 20 minutes at 400°F (200°C). Serve with Khmer Raw Vegetable, Fruit and Herb Plate (page 22).

Serves 4
Preparation time: 45 minutes
Cooking time: 15–20 minutes

# Grilled Pork

In this recipe, a delicious savory-sweet marinade with a rich coconut milk-base imbues tender pork tenderloin with great flavor, making it possible to create a memorable meal with relative ease.

**3 cloves garlic, crushed with the flat side of a cleaver and peeled**
**5 tablespoons soy sauce**
**3 tablespoons palm sugar or dark brown sugar or honey**
**$^2/_3$ cup (150 ml) coconut milk**
**Freshly ground black pepper, to taste**
**14 oz (400 g) lean pork loin, thinly sliced**

Combine the garlic, soy sauce, sugar or honey, coconut milk and black pepper in a shallow dish and mix well. Marinate the pork in this mixture for 1 hour.

Grill the pork over medium heat or roast it in a 400°F (200°C) oven, turning regularly until it's dried and starts to caramelize, about 15 to 20 minutes. Cut into strips and serve with rice and Pickled Vegetables (page 13).

Serves 4
Preparation time: 20 minutes + 1 hour to marinate
Cooking time: 15–20 minutes

# Desserts

In Cambodian sweets tropical ingredients—coconut, palm sugar and bananas—are deftly combined with rice flour, sesame seeds, soybeans or sticky rice, ingredients quintessential to Asia, to create unique and delicious endings to meals or afternoon treats.

# Banana Sesame Fritters

These fritters, more savory than sweet, are often eaten as a snack in Cambodia. Coconut ice cream (page 93) is a popular accompaniment.

5 heaping tablespoons rice flour

2 tablespoons sesame seeds

Pinch of salt

3 tablespoons palm sugar or dark
  brown sugar

3 egg whites

Approximately 1$\frac{1}{4}$ cups (310 ml)
  coconut milk

3 slightly green bananas

Oil, for deep-frying

Serves 4
Preparation time: 30 minutes
Cooking time: 15 minutes

Combine the rice flour, sesame seeds, salt and sugar in a bowl and mix well. Add the egg whites and mix to combine. Gradually add enough coconut milk to produce a thick pancake batter.

Peel one of the bananas and roll it up in the plastic sheet. Place it on a flat surface and press on it by using a heavy pan or a gratin dish to squash the banana until it is flattened—but be careful not to reduce it to a puree. Repeat for each banana.

Heat the oil over high heat in a wok or a deep skillet. When the oil is hot, dip two of the bananas in the batter and then gently lower them into the oil. Deep-fry until crisp and golden then remove and drain on paper towels. Repeat until all the bananas are battered and fried and serve immediately.

# Sticky Rice Cakes with Banana and Coconut

Sticky rice is a short grain rice grown not in water, but on land. In Thailand sticky rice is soaked before steaming, which makes it easy to eat with your fingers. In Cambodia, it is simply steamed which makes it very soft and tender, almost pastelike—and therefore suitable for making desserts.

2 cups (400 g) uncooked glutinous
  rice

1$\frac{3}{4}$ cup (400 ml) coconut milk

4 tablespoons fresh grated or
  unsweetened dried coconut

$\frac{1}{2}$ cup (100 g) sugar

A few banana leaves or aluminum foil

3 very ripe bananas

Makes 8 cakes
Preparation time: 30 mins + 4 hours soaking time
Cooking time: 25 minutes

Soak the rice in cold water for 4 hours. Steam it for 10 minutes; taking care to let it remain slightly firm. While the rice is still warm, mix it with the coconut milk, grated coconut and sugar and set it aside to cool.

If you're using banana leaves, wipe them with a damp cloth and cut them into squares, approximately 10-in (25-cm). Heat a small amount of water in a saucepan and steam the leaves for 3 minutes to soften them. If you're using aluminum foil, cut the foil into the size specified above.

Take one piece of banana leaf or aluminum foil and spread a thin layer of the sticky rice mixture on top. The layer should be approximately the size of one banana, but slightly wider. Place a banana on top of the rice, then spread more rice evenly over the top. Roll up the parcel and secure the ends with wooden toothpicks.

Grill the cakes over medium heat, turning them regularly until the banana leaves start to turn black. Remove from the heat and set aside to cool. To serve, open the banana leaves and slice the rice cakes.

# Sweet Coconut Waffles

Waffles first appeared in Cambodian cuisine during the French colonial period. Rice flour gives them a distinct texture and the combination of coconut milk and palm sugar gives them a highly original flavor.

**2 eggs**
**1$^1/_2$ cup (200 g) rice flour**
**$^1/_2$ cup (125 ml) coconut milk**
**$^1/_2$ cup (100 g) palm sugar or dark brown sugar**
**Pinch of salt**

Preheat and lightly grease a waffle iron.

Break the eggs and separate the whites from the yolks. Combine the rice flour, coconut milk, sugar and egg yolks in a bowl and mix until just combined. Whisk the egg whites with the salt until stiff peaks form and fold gently into the waffle mixture.

Cook the waffles until they are golden brown and crisp.

Serves 4
Preparation time: 25 minutes
Cooking time: 10 minutes

# Palm Sugar Pearls

Cambodians also call this dessert "the cake that kills husbands." Legend has it that certain women would serve this cake (with the sugar inside still boiling hot) to their husband, no doubt when he'd committed some misdeed. The unfortunate husband would swallow the cake but once the outer case dissolved, he'd be horribly burned!

**2 cups (300 g) rice flour**
**Pinch of salt**
**1 cup (200 g) palm sugar or dark brown sugar**
**Warm water**
**4 tablespoons freshly grated or dried unsweetened coconut**

Serves 4
Preparation time: 30 minutes
Cooking time: 20 minutes

Combine the rice flour and salt in a bowl and mix. Gradually add warm water and stir until the mixture has the consistency of modelling clay.

Take a small lump of it and spread it across your fingers to make a disc about 1$^1/_2$-in (3-cm) thick. Put $^1/_2$ teaspoon of the sugar in the center and fold in the edges to completely cover the sugar. Trim any excess pastry and roll the "pearl" in your hands to make a perfect ball. Repeat until all the pastry has been filled and rolled.

Bring a large pot of water of water to a boil and gently lower the pastries into it. They are cooked when they rise to the surface. Remove with a slotted spoon and set aside to cool. Serve sprinkled with the grated coconut.

# Coconut Ice Cream with Caramelized Bananas

The coconut ice cream is a nice accompaniment to Sweet Soybean Cake with Coconut (recipe below).

**Coconut Ice Cream**
1³/₄ cups (400 ml) coconut milk
³/₄ cup (185 ml) sweetened condensed milk
¹/₂ cup (125 ml) light cream
2 tablespoons sugar

**Caramelized Bananas**
2 ripe bananas
4 tablespoons sugar
1 small pinch of salt
1 tablespoon chopped peanuts
¹/₄ cup (60 ml) water

To make the Coconut Ice Cream, combine all the ice cream ingredients and either use an ice cream maker or put the mixture in the freezer, remembering to stir it regularly with a hand mixer or pulse in a food processor.

To make the Caramelized Bananas, peel and roughly mash the bananas. Combine the sugar, salt, peanuts and water in a saucepan and bring to a boil over medium heat. Cook, stirring regularly. Once the mixture starts to caramelize, add the mashed bananas, reduce the heat and mix until the bananas are completely covered and the syrup has slightly reduced. Set aside to cool.

Serve a scoop of the ice cream with a spoonful of the caramelized topping.

Serves 4
Preparation time: 25 minutes plus + 30 minutes for ice cream to set
Cooking time: 15 minutes

# Sweet Soybean Cake with Coconut

This delicacy pairs well with coconut ice cream (above). In Cambodia, there are two types of soybeans: Red or black soybeans, which are mostly used for making soy sauce and tofu; and the green and yellow varieties (the latter are in fact green ones out of the pod), which are used to make cakes once they've been soaked for several hours to make cooking easier. They're available in any Asian grocery or in health food stores.

1¹/₂ cups (150 g) dried yellow soybeans
Pinch of salt
¹/₂ cup (100 g) palm sugar or dark brown sugar
1 cup (250 ml) coconut milk
¹/₂ cup (50 g) freshly grated or dried unsweetened coconut
4 eggs, lightly beaten

Serves 4
Preparation time: 25 minutes + 3 hours to soak the beans
Cooking time: 40 minutes

Put the dried soybeans in a bowl and cover with cold water. Set them aside to soak for at least 3 hours. Drain the beans, put them in a saucepan and cover with fresh water. Bring to a boil and cook for 10 minutes. Drain and set the beans aside.

Combine the salt, sugar, coconut milk, grated coconut and the soybeans in a saucepan over medium heat and gently cook until the beans are soft, stirring constantly. Add the beaten eggs and pour the mixture into a round mold.

Preheat a steamer, and steam the cake for 20 minutes. Set aside to cool before serving.

## The Sala Bai Cooking School

Sala Bai is a tuition-free catering and hotel school founded in 2002 to help impoverished children in Cambodia. Funding comes from both public sources and sponsorship by private organizations. Each year Sala Bai trains about 100 underprivileged young people in four important professions connected with the hotel trade: chef, receptionist, waiter and housekeeper.

Situated in Siem Reap, near the Angkor temples, Sala Bai reaps all the advantages of the thriving tourist trade in that area. When the pupils graduate from the school after eleven months of specialized training, they all, without exception, find a job that will help them support their family.

This book has been produced by volunteers. All of the royalties from sales are paid to the school, thus enabling it to finance more student courses.

## Act for Cambodia

Cambodia was a country at war for many years. Genocide claimed millions of lives and orphaned and deprived many children. Antipersonnel mines still threaten their safety and yet despite these bleak conditions, Cambodian children still smile. If you visit Cambodia, you'll still find people who know how to open their arms in welcome, people for whom the word "family" still means something and for whom solidarity is not just a project but an integral part of daily life. It's a country desperately in need yet so generous that it's impossible to remain indifferent to it.

The French association **Act for Cambodia** founded and now runs the Sala Bai Cooking School. This association has been helping Cambodians since 1984, when it brought aid to the crowds of refugees crossing the borders of Thailand to flee the cruelty of the Khmer Rouge and all the terrible events that struck their nation at that time.

**The association's missions have evolved over time and today they are concentrated in three main areas:**

• Receiving children at the orphanage in Sre Ampil, sending them to school and generally following them through their childhood years;
• Helping rural development through funding, education and training in an isolated province in Northwest Cambodia;
• Providing professional training and guidance for the young people at Sala Bai catering and hotel school.

If you would like to know more about Act for Cambodia and/or make a donation, visit www.actforcambodia.org or write to the following address:

Act for Cambodia USA
712 Union Street
Brooklyn, NY 11215
email: info@actforcambodia.org
telephone: 646-641-1567

# Index

The following photographs were provided by Periplus Publishing: Page 8: top left, top middle column, right column; Page 10: middle column.

Published by Periplus Editions, Ltd.

**www.periplus.com**

© 2005 Agir pour le Cambodge, Joannès Rivière, Maja Smend
First published by Editions Philippe Picquier, France.

ISBN 978-0-7946-5039-1

Distributed by

**North America, Latin America & Europe**
Tuttle Publishing
364 Innovation Drive,
North Clarendon, VT 05759-9436.
Tel: (802) 773-8930; Fax: (802) 773-6993
info@tuttlepublishing.com
www.tuttlepublishing.com

**Japan**
Tuttle Publishing
Yaekari Building, 3rd Floor
5-4-12 Osaki Shinagawa-ku
Tokyo 141 0032
Tel: (81) 03 5437-0171
Fax: (81) 03 5437-0755
sales@tuttle.co.jp
www.tuttle.co.jp

**Asia Pacific**
Berkeley Books Pte Ltd.
61 Tai Seng Avenue
#02-12, Singapore 534167.
Tel: (65) 6280-1330; Fax: (65) 6280-6290
inquiries@periplus.com.sg
www.periplus.com

Printed in Singapore    1207CP

15 14 13 12   5 4 3 2